CENGAGE Learning

Novels for Students, Volume 4 Copyright Notice

Since this page cannot legibly accommodate all copyright notices, the acknowledgments constitute an extension of the copyright notice.

While every effort has been made to secure permission to reprint material and to ensure the reliability of the information presented in this publication, Gale Research neither guarantees the accuracy of the data contained herein nor assumes any responsibility for errors, omissions, or discrepancies. Gale accepts no payment for listing; and inclusion in the publication of any organization, agency, institution, publication, service, or individual does not imply endorsement of the editors or publisher. Errors brought to the attention of the publisher and verified to the satisfaction of the publisher will be corrected in future editions.

This publication is a creative work fully protected

Gale Research
27500 Drake Rd.
Farmington Hills, MI 48331-3535

ISBN 0-7876-2115-3
ISSN 1094-3552

Printed in the United States of America.
10 9 8 7 6 5 4 3

A Lesson Before Dying

Ernest J. Gaines

1993

Introduction

Published by Knopf in 1993, *A Lesson Before Dying* is set in Louisiana. Considered a success by readers and critics alike, the appeal for most readers is derived from the intense emotions the story evokes. The author, Ernest Gaines, wants the reader to feel compassion for the young black man, Jefferson, whom jurors convict for a murder he did not commit. Nor can readers ignore the personal struggles of Grant Wiggins as he teaches Jefferson to be a man.

Gaines credits his boyhood experiences for his ability to develop lifelike characters. In an interview with Paul Desruisseaux for the *New York Times Book Review*, Gaines says he learned by "working in the fields, going fishing in the swamps with the older people, and, especially, listening to the people who came to my aunt's house, the aunt who raised me." His attention to the people he loves results in characters that are believable. Alice Walker, in the *New York Times Book Review*, acknowledges Gaines's success with characterization in saying that Gaines "claims and revels in the rich heritage of Southern Black people and their customs; the community he feels with them is unmistakable and goes deeper even than pride.... Gaines is mellow with historical reflection, supple with wit, relaxed and expansive because he does not equate his people with failure."

Gaines's themes reveal universal truths. He demonstrates that racism destroys people; relationships suffer from people's choices; and pride, honor, and manhood can prevail in trying times. While some critics denounce Gaines for his failure to address blacks' difficulties in today's society, his defense is that he writes for all times and all people.

Author Biography

Ernest J. Gaines, EJ for short, was born in the slave area of a Louisiana plantation on January 15, 1933. His father, Manuel, and mother, Adrienne J. (Colar) Gaines, worked as plantation laborers. Gaines's Aunt Augusteen cared for Gaines and his siblings as they grew up in "the Quarters." Gaines's earliest memories reflect times spent on his aunt's front porch listening to her friends' stories. After Gaines learned to read and write, he enjoyed writing letters for his aunt and her elderly friends. Through listening and writing, Gaines grew to understand himself and his people.

Gaines moved to San Francisco, California, with his mother and stepfather when he was fifteen years old. San Francisco offered Gaines a world of new experiences far removed from his aunt's front porch. Most importantly, he discovered libraries in San Francisco and quickly became an avid reader. Homesick for family, friends, and the Southern plantation lifestyle he had known, Gaines read any fiction he could find that was set in his homeland. He discovered that writers often gave the wrong impression of Southern blacks and the lives they led. These writers were white and had no personal experience with the kind of life Gaines knew existed for Southern blacks. He decided then to write those missing stories. He read other authors whose works he admired: Faulkner, Hemingway, Flaubert, and de Maupassant. The Russian writers, though, inspired him the most. Their stories about Russian peasants offered him a model for writing about the people he knew best.

In the meantime, Gaines graduated with a bachelor of arts degree from San Francisco State College in 1957 and completed graduate work at Stanford University in 1959. In 1962, a young black man named James Meredith tried to enter the University of Mississippi Law School, prompting civil rights demonstrations and violence. Gaines admired Meredith for his determination and courage. As a result, Gaines vowed to dedicate himself to writing about the Southern black experience. After returning to Louisiana, Gaines completed his first novel, *Catherine Carmier*. This 1964 success marked the beginning of his writing career.

Drawing from the stories he heard at his aunt's knee, Gaines writes about the people, places, and daily events of the rural South. Critics have always admired his work. They praise his portrayal of realistic characters and his capable handling of emotional themes: racism, personal relationships, social pressures, social change, and others. Jerry H. Bryant summarizes his talent in a comment in the *Iowa Review*. He asserts that his fiction "contains the austere dignity and simplicity of ancient epic, a concern with man's most powerful emotions and the actions that arise from those emotions, and an artistic intuition that carefully keeps such passions and behavior under fictive control. Gaines may be one of our most naturally gifted storytellers."

Before the Jail Visits

A Lesson Before Dying examines the relationship established between two men in a rural Louisiana parish in the 1940s. One man, Jefferson, is convicted of murder and sentenced to die in the electric chair. The other man, Grant Wiggins, is the local schoolteacher.

The book is told from the point of view of Grant. Although he does not attend Jefferson's trial, he is able to give details from it because everybody in their small community has been talking about it. He explains that Jefferson ended up in trouble because he had received a ride from some friends: they stopped at a liquor store before taking him home, and when the friends tried to rob the store a shoot out occurred, leaving both of his friends and the owner of the store, who was white, dead. Panicking, Jefferson took money from the open cash register before fleeing, and the all-white jury found him guilty of both robbery and murder.

His lawyer, in trying to convince the jury to not impose the death penalty, portrayed Jefferson as being subhuman, presenting him as being too stupid to knowingly be guilty of a crime: "What justice would there be to take this life?" he asked them. "Why, I would just as soon put a hog in the electric chair as this." The afternoon that he is sentenced to die, Jefferson's godmother, who raised him, comes to see Grant, to ask him to visit Jefferson in jail before his execution and to educate him. "I don't want them to kill no hog," she explains. "I want a man to go to that chair, on his own two feet."

Grant is hesitant about getting involved, unsure of what he can do to make Jefferson's life any better in the few weeks that he has left, but Jefferson's godmother, Miss Emma Glenn, is close friends with Grant's aunt, Tante Lou, whom he lives with, and she convinces him to do as Miss Emma asks. Before visits can be arranged, Grant is forced to go through the humiliating process of beseeching the sheriff's cousin for the sheriff's permission, and then being interviewed by the sheriff himself, to make sure that he will not cause any "aggravation."

With permission to proceed with regular visits to the prisoner, Grant has two experiences at the school where he works that bring some perspective to his own life. The superintendent of the schools visits, and Grant finds himself acting servile to him, the way a black man is expected to behave toward a white man, in order to assure that his little one-room school will be kept open. Also, he observes the old men who deliver his wood, and then the school children that he sends out to chop the wood: "And I thought to myself, What am I doing? Am I reaching them at all? They are acting exactly as the old men did earlier. They are fifty years younger, maybe more, but doing the same things those old men did who never attended a day of school in their lives. Is this just a vicious circle? Am I doing anything?"

Visits to Jefferson

Grant is reluctant to become involved with Jefferson from the start, and Jefferson is just as reluctant about receiving visitors. The first few visits, Grant comes with Miss Emma, and then he comes alone. Jefferson does not talk when Miss Emma, whom he calls his nannan, is around, but alone with Grant he bitterly asks about the electric chair and says that he is just a hog, while Grant insists that he is a man.

At the same time, Reverend Ambrose starts visiting Jefferson. Tante Lou, Miss Emma and the Reverend all wish that Grant would try to get Jefferson to be more concerned about his soul and getting into heaven, but Grant, though he believes in God, is not willing to promote their religious beliefs. When he talks with his girlfriend, Vivian, Grant expresses his fondest wish would be for them to leave the parish, to leave the South, as almost everyone who grew up in the area and gotten an education has done before, but he feels stuck there because Vivian's divorce is not final (actually, she points out, he left once, to live with his parents in California, but he came back on his own). At the school Christmas pageant, there is only one package under the tree, with a pair of warm socks and a wool sweater for Jefferson, indicating how much the community is thinking about his imminent execution.

After the date for the execution is set at April 8th, the second Friday after Easter, Jefferson becomes a little less bitter, and he becomes even more at ease with his situation when Grant brings him a radio, although the Reverend and the women are upset that he is listening to music when he should be thinking about God. Jefferson agrees to accept a pencil and a pad of paper to write down things that he might want to talk about during their visits. In the meantime, Grant loses some of the detached cool that he has maintained throughout the ordeal, starting a bar fight with a few mulattos who make racist remarks and say that Jefferson should die. Vivian reminds Grant of the danger that he puts her, and all of the people who depend on him, in when he acts recklessly. At their last visit together, Jefferson is still angry about his fate, but he promises to face it with as much calm as he can, for the sake of his nannan.

The Execution and After

Chapter 29 consists of excerpts from Jefferson's diary, written in his uneducated grammar. He describes his fears and his doubts, but also his relief that he has been able to comfort Miss Emma a little, and that she was able to kiss him for the first time. Chapter 30 describes the day of the execution from the points of view of different citizens in the town: those who saw the truck with the electric chair arrive, those who saw it taken into the courthouse, the deputies who were responsible for having Jefferson's head, arm and leg shaved, the people shopping two blocks away who can hear the generator that powers the electric chair, *etc.*

At his school out in the country, Grant has his children kneel in prayer from twelve o'clock until they receive word that the execution is over, just as Vivian earlier said she planned do with her students. The sheriff's deputy, Paul, who had been the only white man to treat him with respect during his visits to the jail, drives out to the school after it is over, bringing Jefferson's diary to him. "I don't know what you're going to say when you go back in there," Paul tells him. "But tell them he was the bravest man in that room today. I'm a witness, Grant Wiggins. Tell them so." Grant suggests that Paul might come back one day and tell them himself, and he responds, "It would be an honor." When he returns to the classroom, Grant, who has been a stern schoolmaster and a reluctant participant in Jefferson's final days, is crying.

Reverend Mose Ambrose

As the plantation church's pastor, Reverend Ambrose ministers to the laborers and their families. Even though he has no formal education, he serves his people with a true dedication to his vocation. He baptizes, marries, and buries them and offers words of hope and encouragement through his preaching and caring. He and Grant Wiggins share the privilege of visits to Jefferson. Devoted to God, Reverend Ambrose worries about not only Jefferson's soul, but also Grant's. He continually tries to talk to Grant about God and encourages Grant to discuss God with Jefferson. He wants to know if Grant has determined Jefferson's deepest feelings about death and what it will mean for his soul. Grant, however, feels that Reverend Ambrose is responsible for preparing Jefferson's soul for death. Reverend Ambrose accuses Grant of being selfish and uneducated because Grant will not accept that heaven exists and will not use his relationship with Jefferson to get Jefferson to accept salvation. Reverend Ambrose believes Grant is a lost soul.

Vivian Baptiste

Vivian is Grant Wiggins's girlfriend, even though she is still married. A beautiful woman, she draws attention to herself wherever she goes. She has light skin, long black hair, high cheekbones, and greenish-brown eyes. She stands tall—about five foot seven—and dresses well. When Tante Lou and Miss Emma first meet her, they resent her light skin and the fact that Vivian seldom visits her parents. They change their minds about her, however, when they learn that she regularly attends church. They call her a "lady of quality." Grant knows that Vivian is a lady. Also a teacher, Vivian understands Grant and his desire to move elsewhere to teach and to see more of the world. Grant turns to Vivian for solace during the trying months of his relationship with Jefferson.

Bear

Bear is one of the two boys who pick Jefferson up on their way to Mr. Grope's store. Bear does all the talking. Not only does he ask and plead for the liquor, he also takes the first steps around the counter toward Mr. Grope. Bear and his friend, Brother, die in the altercation, along with Mr. Grope.

Paul Bonin

Paul is the young deputy at the jail. When Miss Emma asks the older deputy how Jefferson is, and the older deputy says, "Quiet," Miss Emma mistakes the response for a command that she be quiet. Paul quickly sees what has happened and answers her question with "Jefferson's been quiet," which relieves the tension. Paul speaks civilly to both Miss Emma and Grant, not ordering them to do something, but asking them politely. For example, after checking Grant's pockets to make sure they are empty, Paul tells Grant that he can put his things back into his pockets. Paul is a white man with brown hair and gray-blue eyes and is a little younger than Grant. Paul takes Grant to Jefferson's cell each time Grant visits. As they see more of one another, Paul and Grant establish a sort of friendship, with Paul showing his sincere concern for Jefferson's fate. Paul hates having to search Grant when he visits and lets Grant know that he only does it because it is a matter of policy. Paul witnesses Jefferson's death and tries to tell Grant that he has done a good job as a teacher. Even though Paul and Grant do not agree on matters of faith, Paul tells Grant that he wants to be his friend.

Brother

Brother is one of the two boys who pick Jefferson up on their way to Mr. Grope's store. When a fight breaks out among Mr. Grope, Bear, and Brother, all three die.

Joe Claiborne

Joe Claiborne runs the Rainbow Club bar and is married to Thelma. He drives a new white Cadillac and allows customers to buy on credit when they need to. Friends gather at the Club to talk and drink. Grant visits the club often because he feels wanted there, and it is a place where he and Vivian can dance and be together.

Thelma Claiborne

Thelma Claiborne runs the Rainbow Club cafe and is married to Joe. She has a smile full of gold teeth and wears strong perfume. People can depend on Thelma for good food and friendly conversation.

Irene Cole

Irene Cole serves as Grant's student teacher and assists him with the younger students. Even though Grant can not see it, Irene harbors a secret love for him.

Emma Glenn

See Emma Nannan

Alcee Grope

Grope is the white storeowner whom Jefferson is accused of killing. Grope likes Jefferson and asks about his nannan. When the two boys Jefferson is with ask for liquor, Grope refuses to give it to them because they do not have enough money to pay for it. The two boys are already drunk. A fight ensues, and Grope and the two boys are all dead when it is over.

Sam Guidry

Sam Guidry, the sheriff, always tries to put Grant Wiggins in his place. He expects Grant to behave like a subordinate, telling Grant when Grant uses proper grammar and speaks intelligently that he's too smart for his own good. As the sheriff, Guidry runs the jail, but he is seldom present when Grant visits. When he is on duty, Guidry looks like a cowboy; he wears a Stetson hat and cowboy boots. His appearance can intimidate people, though. Guidry has a strong face and large hands, and is tall and tanned. Guidry thinks that Grant's teaching Jefferson is a joke; he believes Jefferson is not only guilty of the crime, but stupid as well.

Mr. Henri

See Henri Pichot

Jefferson

A twenty-one-year-old slightly retarded black man, Jefferson has always lived on the Pichot plantation with his godmother, Miss Emma, or "Nannan," as he calls her. On his way to a bar one October day, Jefferson accepts a ride from two other young black men, Bear and Brother. Bear and Brother decide to stop to buy liquor but have no money between them. The two think the store owner, Mr. Grope, will allow them to get the liquor on credit. When they ask him, he disagrees, and they begin to argue. Already drunk, Bear starts around the counter. Mr. Grope gets his gun and begins to shoot. Before Jefferson knows what has happened, all three men are dead. Confused, he is still in the store when two white men find him. He gets blamed for robbing and killing the storeowner.

Jefferson's attorney tries to use Jefferson's mental disability as a defense, claiming he has no more intelligence than a hog. The white jury, however, finds Jefferson guilty, and the judge sentences him to the electric chair. Miss Emma resents Jefferson's being labeled a hog, and implores Grant Wiggins to teach him enough that he can walk to the electric chair with some pride.

When Wiggins begins his visits, Jefferson greets him with silence, the whites of his eyes bloodshot. Jefferson later replaces his silence with talk full of self-disgust and a sense of hopelessness. After months of visits, though, Jefferson begins to question Wiggins about God and heaven, his nannan, and life. Wiggins brings Jefferson a radio; they share a favorite announcer. He also gives Jefferson a notebook. Jefferson writes in the notebook until his death on Good Friday in April. From their conversations during Jefferson's last days and the journal Jefferson has kept, Wiggins learns that to be a teacher, one has to believe. He concludes that Jefferson is the true teacher.

Inez Lane

The current cook at the plantation's big house, Inez greets Miss Emma, Tante Lou, and Grant each time they visit Henri Pichot. She wears the white dress and shoes of a cook, with a blue gingham apron and kerchief on her head. Inez suffers for her friends when Mr. Pichot and his friends keep them waiting. She says little but continues her duties serving the head of the household and his white visitors.

Media Adaptations

- An unabridged audio version of *A Lesson Before Dying*, read by Jay Long, is a 1997 Random House production (ISBN: 0375402586).

- Juneteenth Audio Books offers an abridged edition of *A Lesson Before Dying* produced by Time Warner Audio Books (ISBN: 1570422230).

Tante Lou

Tante Lou, Grant Wiggins's aunt, raised him. She is also Miss Emma's best friend, having worked with her in the big Pichot house as a washerwoman. A large person like Miss Emma, Tante Lou keeps Grant in line with her stern nature and her devout faith. She hates that Grant does not attend church or admit to believing in God. She avoids him entirely on Sundays. She expects Grant to visit and teach Jefferson because it is what she and Miss Emma want him to do. Tante Lou is the one who sent Wiggins to the university to make a better life for himself and the people around him. As a result, Tante Lou believes that Wiggins is obligated to do what he can for Jefferson.

Miss Emma Nannan

To Jefferson, Miss Emma is "Nannan," his godmother and the person who loves and has raised him. Although in her seventies, Miss Emma strikes a formidable appearance. She weighs nearly two hundred pounds and commands respect from everyone she knows. Even her late husband called her Miss Emma. Miss Emma used to cook for the plantation owner, Henri Pichot. She pins her gray hair to the top of her head and often sports a wellworn brown felt hat and overcoat with rabbit fur trimming the collar and sleeves. She knows that Jefferson has limited intelligence but wants him to learn to read and write before he dies. More importantly, she wants him to understand that he is a man and not the "hog" the court says he is. A religious woman, Miss Emma prays for Jefferson's soul and relies on Reverend Ambrose for spiritual guidance for her and Jefferson.

Henri Pichot

A medium-sized man with long white hair, Henri Pichot owns the plantation on which Grant's school is located and where Miss Emma, Jefferson, Tante Lou, and Grant live. As the plantation owner, Mr. Pichot lives in its main house, a large structure containing modern amenities available to the wealthy. Mr. Pichot begrudgingly meets with Miss Emma, Tante Lou, and Grant to hear Miss Emma's request to allow Grant to visit Jefferson in his jail cell. Pichot only allows the visit because Miss Emma used to work for him. Mr. Pichot is the sheriff's brother-in-law, so Miss Emma thinks that Mr. Pichot might be able to convince the sheriff to permit Wiggins's visits to the jail. Although Pichot quickly dismisses Miss Emma and her friends on their first visit, he appears to become more sympathetic to their cause as time goes on.

Louis Rougon

Henri Pichot's cohort, Louis Rougon owns the bank close to the plantation. He is present each time Grant visits the plantation house and wears the clothes of a successful businessman: gray suit, white shirt, and gray-and-white-striped tie. Rougon thinks it is amusing that Miss Emma wants Grant to teach Jefferson and smirks his thoughts in Grant's presence.

Mr. Sam

See Sam Guidry

Grant Wiggins

Grant Wiggins, the teacher, grew up on the Pichot plantation. Tante Lou, Grant's aunt and the plantation's washerwoman, raised him. Even though Tante Lou earned a living in the plantation's main house, she did not want Grant to have to enter the house ever again through the back door, the servant's entrance. Thus, she sacrificed to send him to the university to become a teacher, a respected member of society.

At the opening of the story, Grant has taught at the plantation school for six years. The school has not changed much since he left it ten years earlier, nor have the children changed. He knows the children and their families well. He knows which children will fail and which will succeed. He understands their family situations. He encourages the children to do the best they can and to help one another. The community, in turn, appreciates Grant's returning to the plantation to teach reading and writing. It is because Grant remains one of them, yet has the education no one else has, that Miss Emma chooses him to visit and teach Jefferson. Jefferson has just been convicted of killing the white storeowner and awaits his death. Grant is to try to teach Jefferson to be a man—to try to instill in him a sense of self-worth and pride.

Grant doubts first, his ability to reach Jefferson, and later, his ability to teach him anything of value. He feels frustrated with himself and angry with the system. Grant sees the injustice around him and realizes that he can do nothing to change it. For example, when Grant faces the sheriff or Henri Pichot, he knows that they expect him to act the part of a slave, bowing to their demands. This disturbs him so much that at one point, he fights a man for the hateful comments the man makes about Jefferson. When Grant needs understanding, he turns to Vivian Baptiste, his girlfriend. While Miss Emma, Reverend Ambrose, and Tante Lou would like for Grant to help Jefferson find God, Grant knows that he is the wrong one to help Jefferson with this. Grant questions his own beliefs and is unable to assure Jefferson of heaven. In the end, Grant believes that Reverend Ambrose and Jefferson are the real teachers. Grant takes no credit for having prepared Jefferson to face death and feels a great sadness for the realization and for the loss of Jefferson's life.

Themes

Justice and Injustice

From the beginning until the very end of *A Lesson Before Dying* a sense of injustice prevails. While this theme derives from the larger theme of racism, Gaines uses specific incidents to demonstrate how underlying racist beliefs can result in miscarriage of justice. Jefferson innocently accepts a ride with two conniving young men who are planning to take advantage of a white businessman. When the three other men die in the resulting struggle, Jefferson, who is slightly retarded, does not really understand what has happened or even remember how he got there. Unfairly accused by two white men who come into the store and find Jefferson leaving with money and whiskey in his pockets, Jefferson is later tried and convicted for the crime and sentenced to die in the electric chair. The injustice continues after Jefferson is jailed, and it extends to the people he loves. Tante Lou, the Reverend, and Grant Wiggins suffer ill treatment when they try to arrange visitation and each time that they visit Jefferson thereafter. The intolerance shown by the white accusers, jurors, judge, and jailers results from their racist belief that they are superior to black people.

Civil Rights and Racism

The story takes place in the late 1940s when the country's Civil Rights movement was moving towards integration. Integration enables equal rights to all people, allowing them to live together in harmony regardless of their race or skin color. In the South, however, during the time this novel is set, segregation still reigns. Segregation, the opposite of integration, separates races. Racism results when one race views itself as superior over another and determines that it should have more rights than the other. This view held true in the South, particularly on the large plantations where many blacks labored for white landowners. Whites considered blacks inferior human beings. Whites did not want to associate with blacks in any way. Gaines provides clear examples of racist behavior and the varying effects racist behaviors have on people's lives.

In *A Lesson Before Dying* whites treat Jefferson unfairly through their actions, their words, and their attitudes. Not only are people inconsiderate of Jefferson, they also disenfranchise Jefferson's friends and family. For example, when his nannan, Miss Emma, Tante Lou, and Grant Wiggins visit Mr. Pichot, they must enter through the kitchen. They are expected to remain there until Mr. Pichot and his associates summon them, which was, in one case, two hours later. Mr. Pichot and his companions also expect Grant Wiggins to act a certain way because he is black. Even though they know Wiggins is an educated man, they make it clear to him that he should mumble, use improper grammar, and not meet them eye-to-eye.

Topics for Further Study

- Define capital punishment. Trace its history since ancient times. Discuss the reforms introduced throughout the ages to eliminate the use of capital punishment.

- Research capital punishment. Take a position for or against it. Prepare to defend your position in a classroom debate.

- Critics refer to Gaines as a master storyteller. He, himself, credits others for the stories they told when he was growing up and that he has borrowed. In other words, the "oral tradition" greatly influences his writing. Describe the relative importance of the tradition in various cultures and explain the purposes the tradition serves for different peoples.

- Even though is set in the late 1940s, racism still exists in the small town of Bayonne. Trace the history of the Civil Rights movement. Relate your findings to the fictional events that occur in the story.

Not only did racism exist between the blacks and whites, but also between the blacks and mulattos. The mulattos were of mixed black and European heritage. They refused to work side-by-side on the plantations with "niggers" and became bricklayers instead. Grant Wiggins fights two of them at the Rainbow Club one night when he hears them making derogatory comments about Jefferson and making light of Jefferson's impending death.

While racism abounds in the story, destroying people's lives along the way, one equitable relationship between a black man and a white man blossoms to serve as a beacon of hope for the future. Grant Wiggins and Paul Bonin forge the beginnings of a friendship. Paul, the young white deputy at the jail, sees beyond the color of Jefferson's skin and feels compassion for his situation. He appreciates, too, the part Grant Wiggins plays in trying to make the rest of Jefferson's life, and the thought of his upcoming death, more bearable. Paul tries to treat Wiggins with respect. He shows a deference for his education as well as his consideration for Jefferson and his nannan. When he speaks to Wiggins, he looks him in the eye and encourages Wiggins to do the same. He completes the required weapons searches on Wiggins less thoroughly than he might on someone he does not know or trust. Wiggins feels the same way about Paul. Wiggins understands that he and Paul have an appreciation for one another, although Wiggins does not feel worthy of Paul's. In the end, Paul compliments Wiggins on his teaching talent, even though Wiggins does not agree that he deserves the compliment. Paul tells Wiggins that he would like to be his friend.

God and Religion

Jefferson's relationship with God, and his understanding of faith, heaven, and salvation concern Miss Emma, Tante Lou, and Reverend Ambrose. Miss Emma and Tante Lou think that Wiggins's visits to Jefferson will prepare Jefferson to die with some dignity. They think that Wiggins, with his education, knows what it will take to instill in Jefferson some sense of self-worth. They believe that Wiggins can tell what Jefferson's deepest thoughts are about life and his upcoming death. When Wiggins gives Jefferson a radio, Reverend Ambrose, Tante Lou, and Miss Emma are appalled, calling it a box of sin and telling Wiggins that Jefferson needs God in his cell rather than a disembodied radio announcer. Wiggins tells them that he himself is not the one to provide Jefferson with spiritual guidance, admitting that he questions heaven's existence and God's love.

Jefferson, too, struggles with faith issues until his dying day, wondering if God loves only white people. Yet, he walks to the chair a man rather than an unsure, beaten-down slave. Paul credits Wiggins's teaching for the transformation. Wiggins sarcastically attributes it to God's work.

Setting

Gaines sets *A Lesson Before Dying* in and around the fictitious Bayonne, a small town in Louisiana. It is 1948. Some events occur on the plantation, either in the school where Grant Wiggins teaches or in the homes of Henri Pichot, Tante Lou, or Miss Emma. Other events occur at the jail or at the Rainbow Club.

The church serves as the school for the black children whose parents labor on the plantation. There are no desks; the children write on their laps or kneel in front of the benches that are pews on Sundays. Grant Wiggins's desk is the collection table during church services. A woodburning stove for which there is never enough fuel heats the classroom. The same sparseness exists in the homes of both Tante Lou and Miss Emma. Tante Lou shares her small home with Wiggins. The furniture is old, and the wallpaper peels away from the walls. While Tante Lou has added her own homey touches, the house has a tired feeling to it. Wiggins refers to it as "rustic." Miss Emma's home is even smaller, with the bed in the living room. Henri Pichot's house, however, is a huge house with modern appliances. Instead of a woodburning stove, the cook uses a gas range for cooking. The same black iron pots that Wiggins remembers from childhood hang on the wall, but the old icebox he had known has been replaced by a sparkling white refrigerator.

The important events of the story take place in the jail. The jail is located in the old redbrick courthouse that resembles a castle. Housing both black and white prisoners in different areas, the cells themselves are located on the second floor of the courthouse, at the top of a set of steel stairs. The cells of the other African-American prisoners have two metal bunks each. Jefferson's, however, has only one bunk, equipped with a mattress and wool blanket. A toilet, a washbowl, and a small metal shelf take up the rest of the six-foot by ten-foot cell. For light, there is only a single light bulb hanging from the center of the ceiling and a small, high, barred window.

Wiggins goes to the Rainbow Club for company and comfort. Green, yellow, and red neon lights advertise the combination bar and cafe. In the bar, Wiggins can choose to sit on a barstool at the counter or at one of the white-clothed tables in the dimly lit room. The cafe boasts both a lunch counter and tables with cheery red-and-white-checkered tablecloths.

Point of View

Gaines uses the first person point of view to tell the story of Grant Wiggins. That is, Wiggins tells the story himself as the events affect him. By using his voice, Gaines can easily portray the intense emotions that Wiggins feels in relationship to the other characters and the struggles they endure. The resulting narrative enables Gaines to connect his fiction with historical reality. Gaines shares his own life experiences and perceptions with his readers through the lives and emotions of his characters. He aptly weaves fact and fiction to present his reflections on the Southern world that he knows existed. A twist to the typical personal narrative, though, is Jefferson's journal. Reading the entries, Wiggins knows Jefferson's innermost thoughts. By definition, a first-person narrator does not know what another character is thinking.

Style

Critics often compare Gaines's stories to epics. Although epics are usually in the form of long narrative poems, there are similarities between the two: both describe extraordinary achievements or events; and both have epic characters that stand heroic in the face of large-scale deeds. In the case of Wiggins, there is no hope that he can save Jefferson from the death that he will suffer as a result of a society's large-scale racist beliefs. Yet, Wiggins does help Jefferson gain self respect before he dies, in spite of the efforts of those who would persecute Jefferson for his skin color. Paul Bonin views Wiggins as a hero even if Wiggins, himself, does not.

Black Civil Rights in the Late 19th Century

With the Emancipation Proclamation of 1863, President Lincoln freed the slaves. Congressional Acts after that date granted blacks various civil rights. In 1866 and 1870, blacks received the rights to sue, be sued, and own property. With these rights, blacks gained the "privileges" of white citizens. The Fourteenth Amendment to the Constitution, in 1868, further extended black privileges, making former slaves eligible for citizenship. The Fifteenth Amendment gave blacks the right to vote and prevented state or federal governments from denying any citizen of this right on the basis of race. Blacks received further acceptance through the Civil Rights Act of 1871, which made it a crime to deny citizens of equal protection under the law, and the Civil Rights Act of 1875, which guaranteed blacks the right to use public accommodations.

The political climate in the United States shifted in the mid-1880s, however, to an attitude of indifference towards social justice. The Civil Rights Act of 1875 (right to public accommodations) was declared unconstitutional. Then, the Supreme Court legally instituted segregation through its decision in the case of Plessy v. Ferguson in 1896. Homer

Plessy had been arrested and convicted for refusing to sit in a railroad car that was designated for African Americans. When he appealed his conviction on the grounds that it denied him his rights under the Thirteenth and Fourteenth Amendments, the Supreme Court overruled him. The Court upheld the principle of "separate but equal" facilities for blacks and whites. Even into the 1930s when Ernest Gaines was born, this principle and attitude towards blacks prevailed. Gaines set *A Lesson Before Dying* in the late 1940s, but the remnants of segregation still existed. The jail where Jefferson was incarcerated had a separate block of cells for African-American inmates, in addition to separate restroom facilities for African-American visitors to the jail.

Segregation in the South

Taking a step backwards after the Supreme Court's decision in the Plessy case, integration seemed impossible. Segregation was well established in the Northern states through custom rather than law. This was known as "de facto" segregation. Following the Plessy case, however, the South decreed laws that legalized racial segregation. This legal segregation is called "de jure" segregation. The laws that accomplished de jure segregation in the South are known as the Jim Crow laws, named after a pre-Civil War minstrel show character. These laws create a racial caste system in the South that held strong until 1954, when the Supreme Court declared public-school segregation unconstitutional in the Brown v. Board of Education case in Topeka, Kansas.

Early Steps Towards Integration in the 20th Century

The early 1900s saw steps being taken towards integration through two movements. One group worked towards equal treatment through integration; the other group wanted to establish a separate black state. In 1909, W. E. B. Du Bois founded the National Association for the Advancement of Colored People (NAACP). The NAACP still exists today and works for equality through integration. Another leader in the integration movement was Marcus Garvey, who founded the Universal Negro Improvement Association (UNIA) in 1914 to work towards a separate black state through black nationalism. While the UNIA no longer exists, the black nationalist movement continues.

Efforts to integrate continued to progress through the 1930s and 1940s. Black leaders found powerful support in black unions such as the Brotherhood of Sleeping Car Porters who helped apply economic pressure to pass such acts as the 1947 Fair Employment Practices Act. This legislation prevented discrimination in hiring on the basis of race or national origin. In 1948, Harry Truman ordered the integration of the armed forces. These early efforts to end segregation culminated in the Supreme Court ruling in the 1954 Brown v.

Board of Education case. The ruling declared separate schools for blacks and whites unconstitutional.

Critical Overview

Gaines' sixth novel, *A Lesson Before Dying*, provides more support for his reputation as a talented writer. Since the 1964 publication of *Catherine Carmier*, his writing has served to present African-American culture in the same authentic light as the stories shared orally by the people who have lived them. Reading the stories of Ernest Gaines nearly equals having the experiences.

Critics agree that Gaines has a true sense of characterization. He asserts that his characters appear realistic because he has shaped them from people he knew while growing up on a Louisiana plantation. He cites the influence of Russian writers on his characterization. Russian writers relate stories about their peasant countrymen in a way that is caring, yet not cloying. These writers present truths without being harsh or disapproving. Gaines presents his people, his characters, in this same manner. He describes Southern blacks as he knows they truly are, not as they are represented in stories he read as a young man. The characters he encountered in those books were foreign to him. After failing to find accurate stories about his people, he decided to write them himself. Gaines told Joseph McLellan in the *Washington Post*, "If the book you want doesn't exist, you try to make it exist." The strength of his characters complements his exceptional writing. Just as "a swimmer cannot influence the flow of a river ..." says Larry

McMurtry in the *New York Times Book Review*, "the characters of Ernest Gaines … are propelled by a prose that is serene, considered and unexcited."

Gaines's "serene" prose belies the serious nature of his writing. Part of the appeal of his work lies in the way that he handles life's intense themes in his stories. In fact, his stories do not always have happy endings. Gaines presents truths in his novels; critics applaud this. They commend him, for example, for confronting the tough issues that destroy relationships among people, yet build character and strength. His characters often struggle with questions that test their belief systems and pit friends or family members against one another. To illustrate, in one story, a young woman must choose between her father and her lover, a choice forced by the racial and social differences between them. In others, characters search for human dignity and pride. They face alienation and loneliness as well. As an example, both Jefferson and Wiggins experience isolation and desolation in *A Lesson Before Dying*. Yet the story really honors man's natural instinct to persevere in the face of adversity. This is demonstrated in Jefferson's learning the lessons that enable him to walk to his death with a sense of who he really is.

Reviewers often compare his writing to William Faulkner's. The story for example, takes place on a plantation near the small, imaginary town of Bayonne, Louisiana. This region compares to Faulkner's Yoknapatawpha County, a fictional county in rural Mississippi. Like Faulkner, Gaines created the place and its people from experiences and relationships he actually had as a child. Another comparison made between Gaines's and Faulkner's writing has to do with the characters the two writers portray. Faulkner writes about two families. One, the Sartoris family, boasts years of wealthy prominence in the community. The other, the newly rich Snopes family, lacks the social graces of people born into the area's aristocracy. Gaines aristocracy and "lesser quality" people are the southern white plantation owners and the Cajuns, respectively. The plantation owners, although French descendants themselves, consider themselves a higher class than the Cajuns, who are direct descendants of Canadian French. Of even lesser nobility, according to the southern class structure, are the blacks and the Creoles. The Creoles are often of mixed black and European heritage and referred to as mulattos. As do Faulkner's works, his stories reveal the complex socioeconomic interactions among his characters but even more explicitly point out the relationships between the blacks and whites.

Critics agree that his African-American heritage lends a uniquely original perspective to his stories. According to Alvin Aubert in his essay in *Contemporary Novelists*, "Gaines's peculiar point of view generates a more complex social vision than Faulkner's, an advantage Gaines has sustained with dramatic force and artistic integrity."

Sources

Alvin Aubert, "Ernest J. Gaines: Overview," in *Contemporary Novelists, 6th ed.*, edited by Susan Windisch Brown, St. James Press, 1996.

Jerry H. Bryant, *Iowa Review*, Winter, 1972.

Paul Desruisseaux, in *New York Times Book Review*, May 23, 1971.

Joseph McLellan, in *Washington Post*, January 13, 1976.

Larry McMurtry, in *New York Times Book Review*, November 19, 1967.

Alice Walker, in *New York Times Book Review*, October 30, 1983.

For Further Study

Alvin Aubert, "Ernest J. Gaines: Overview," in *Contemporary Novelists, 6th ed.*, edited by Susan Windisch Brown, St. James Press, 1996.

> The author provides not only points of comparison between the work of Gaines and Faulkner, but also an overview of how black-white relationships become the basic element in each of Gaines's novels.

H. A. Baker, and P. Redmond, P, editors, *AfroAmerican Literary Study in the 1990's (Black Literature and Culture)*, University of Chicago Press, 1989.

> This is first in a series of volumes dedicated to the scholarly study of African-American literature and culture.

B. Bell, "African American Literature," in *Grolier Multimedia Encyclopedia [CD-ROM]*, Grolier Interactive, Inc., 1998.

> An explanation of the tradition of African-American literature and its attributes. The author explains the effects of race, ethnicity, class, gender, and nationality on literature and discusses African-American literature in terms of genres and their

contributing writers.

J. Dizard, "Racial Integration," in *Grolier Multimedia Encyclopedia [CD-ROM]*, Grolier Interactive, Inc., 1998.

> The author defines and gives the history of racial integration in the United States and provides references to Civil Rights acts of particular importance.

D. C. Estes, *Critical Reflections on the Fiction of Ernest J. Gaines*, University of Georgia Press (Athens), 1994.

> This series of essays provides a comprehensive look at Gaines's work, including the themes he addresses, the techniques he uses, and his use of humor. The author also presents comparisons to other writers' works.

R. Laney, *Ernest J. Gaines: Louisiana Stories*, Video Production by Louisiana Public Broadcasting, Louisiana Educational Television Authority. [Online] Available http://oscar.lpb.org/programs/gaines/, 1998.

> This video production provides viewers with an overview of the life of Ernest Gaines. Through interviews with Gaines, his lifetime acquaintances, and prominent writers and scholars, the viewer will come to

an appreciation of Gaines and the influences on his writing.

V. Smith, and A. Walton, editors, *African American Writer*, Charles Scribner Sons, 1991.

A compilation of essays that are a combination of biography and literary criticism. They focus on the unique experiences of African Americans and their culture and tradition in the context of American history.

CPSIA information can be obtained
at www.ICGtesting.com
Printed in the USA
BVHW041052170620
581539BV00007B/687